GENERATIONS

BABY BOOMERS 1950–1963

> Take the 3,548,000 babies born in 1950. Bundle them into a batch, bounce them all over the bountiful land that is America. What do you get? Boom. The biggest, boomiest boom ever known in history.
>
> —Sylvia Porter
> *New York Post* (May 4, 1951)

Produced by
Alfred Music Publishing Co., Inc.
P.O. Box 10003
Van Nuys, CA 91410-0003
alfred.com

Printed in USA.

ISBN-10: 0-7390-6550-5

ISBN-13: 978-0-7390-6550-1

Cover Photos:
© istockphoto/anzeletti, biffspandex, eliadric, GeofferyHolman, hundreddays, Imagesbybarbara, ParentesiGrafica, schlot
© stock.xchng/andrewatla, deebeee999, lxine, suzula, mattosense

FOREWORD

The term "baby boomers" immediately brings to mind a mix of significant events and issues: the Civil Rights Movement, the assassination of President John Fitzgerald Kennedy, the Vietnam War, the birth of "suburbia," Woodstock, feminism, free love, and more. The baby boom generation witnessed, and initiated, some of the pivotal moments in American history.

After World War II ended in 1945, thousands of soldiers returned home to the United States ready to begin their adult lives. Bolstered by a strong economy and the far-reaching GI Bill, which made homes affordable, young couples saw a chance to live the American Dream, which had been shadowed by the Great Depression and the war. Starting a family was central to this dream. In stark contrast to the low birth rates during the war, from 1946 to 1964 the country experienced the highest birth rates and fastest population growth ever. At the end of the boom, almost half of the population was under the age of 25. From the cities to the newly formed suburbs, the baby boomers were destined to change America—through sheer size alone.

Music was prominent during this change, becoming central to the generation. Their favorite songs—"bubblegum" pop, rock and roll, and even protest songs—can be found in the two volumes of *Generations: Baby Boomers*. The first volume explores hits from 1950 to 1963, the music that boomers heard during childhood. These songs both shaped their early years and became the basis for their later rebellions. This music captures the innocent style of the 1950s, such as the catchy and squeaky-clean songs *Sixteen Candles* (The Crests) and *Only You (And You Alone)* (The Platters). There are songs in the "doo-wop" style, which featured tight vocal harmonies and nonsense syllables, such as the hits *A Teenager In Love* (Dion and the Belmonts) and *Blue Moon* (The Marcels). There are also timeless standards, such as *It Was a Very Good Year*, which was made famous by Frank Sinatra. There are also the first inklings of popular music becoming a lightning rod for action and experimentation. Bob Dylan revolted against war in *Blowin' in the Wind,* in which he asked a series of questions about the nature of man in the modern world. *Puff (The Magic Dragon)* became a theme song for recreational drug use, despite author Peter Yarrow's adamant denial that the song had any such connotations.

The baby boomer generation is unique in American history; it is doubtful that such a sudden and protracted population increase will happen again. This collection is designed to spark nostalgic memories for those who grew up during that time. For new players, it is an introduction to this great music. Enjoy discovering or revisiting this important time in the history of popular music, the music of the *Baby Boomers!*

Each piece in this collection has been carefully arranged for intermediate to late intermediate pianists. Lyrics are also included as well as suggestions for fingering, pedaling, and phrasing.

TABLE OF CONTENTS

All I Have to Do Is Dream

Words and Music by
Boudleaux Bryant
Arranged by Melody Bober

6

On - ly trou - ble is, gee whiz, I'm dream-ing my life____ a -

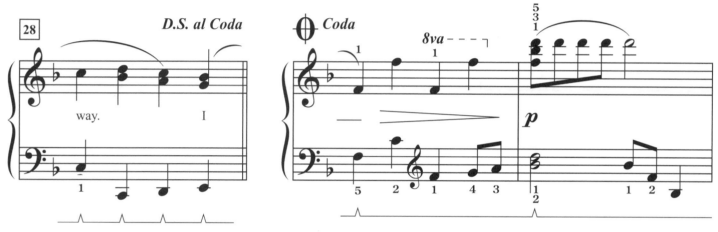

D.S. al Coda   **Coda**

way.   I

8va - - - -

p

mp

Blowin' in the Wind

Words and Music by Bob Dylan
Arranged by Melody Bober

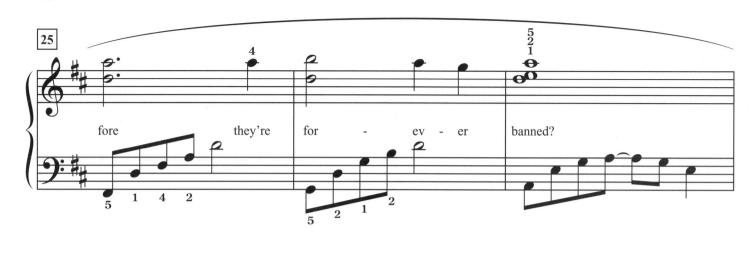

fore   they're   for - ev - er   banned?

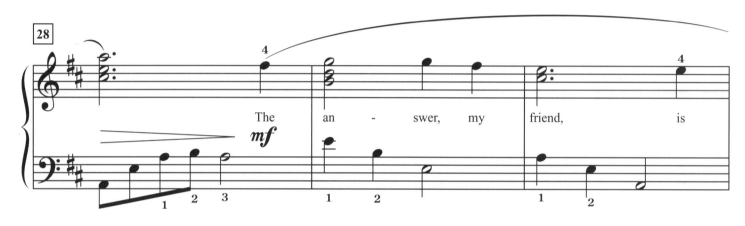

The   an - swer, my   friend,   is

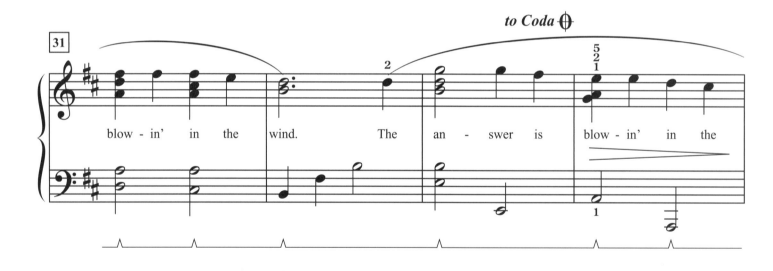

blow - in' in the   wind.   The   an - swer is   blow - in' in the

to Coda

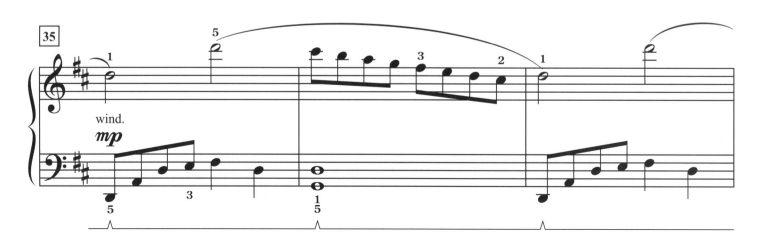

wind.

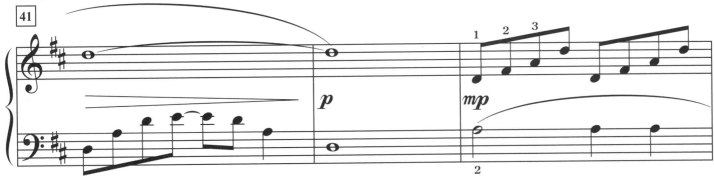

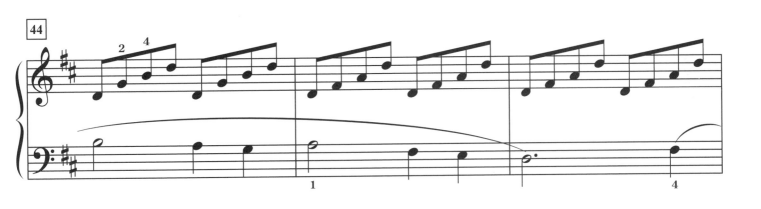

12

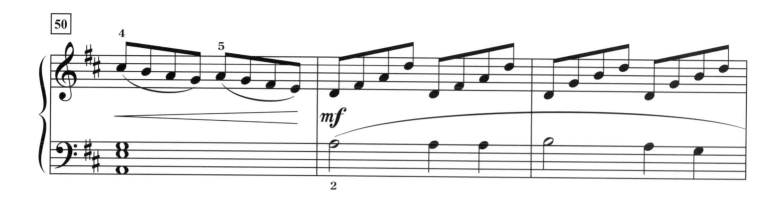

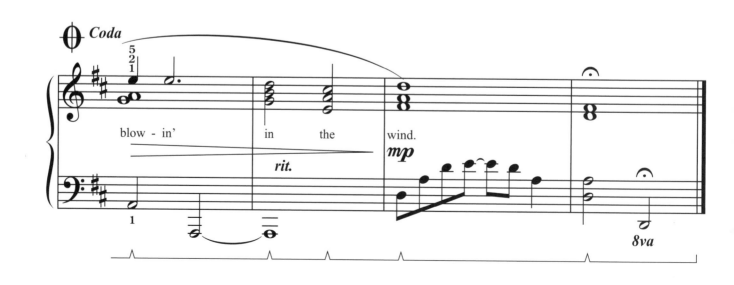

Blue Velvet

Words and Music by
Lee Morris and Bernie Wayne
Arranged by Melody Bober

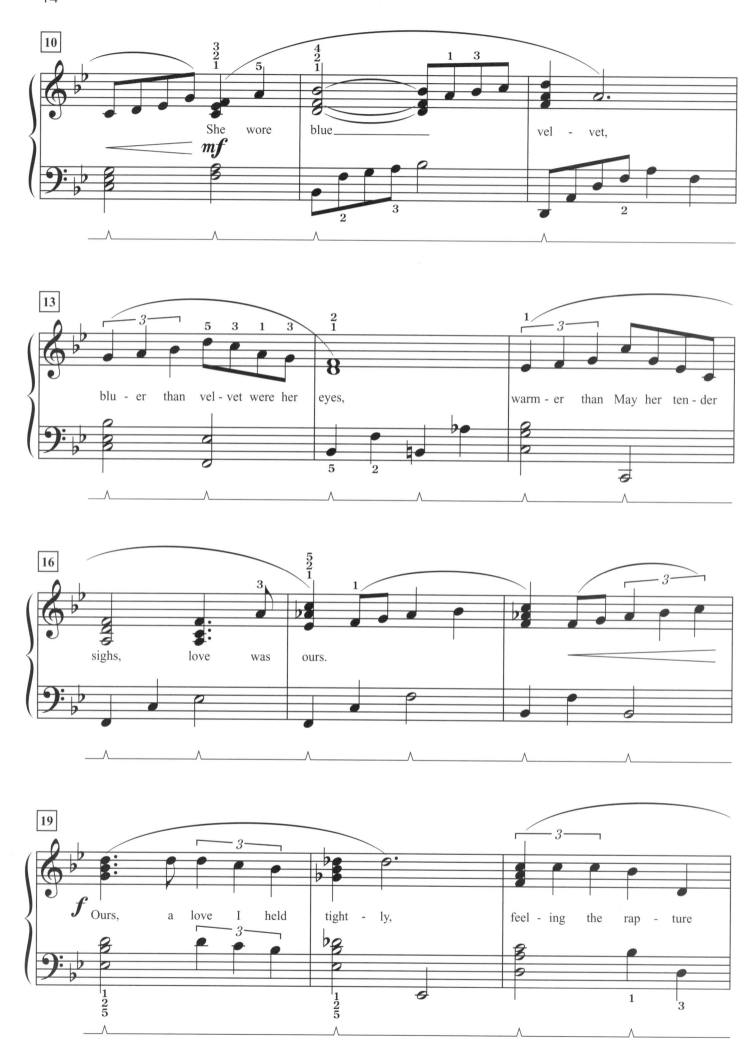

and I still can see blue vel - vet through my

tears.

Blue Moon

Music by Richard Rodgers
Lyrics by Lorenz Hart
Arranged by Melody Bober

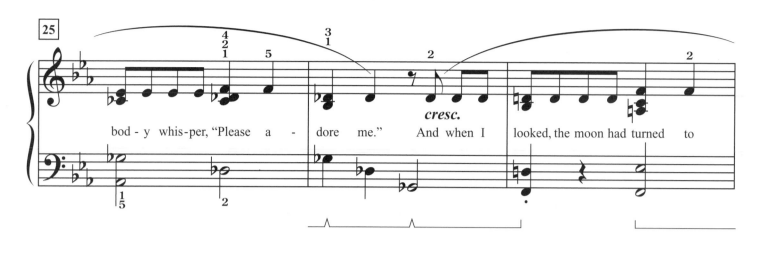

bod - y whis-per, "Please a - dore me." And when I looked, the moon had turned to

cresc.

gold! Blue___ moon, now I'm no long - er a -

f

lone with-out a dream in my heart,

___ *simile*

with-out a love of my own.

p

Bye Bye Love

Words and Music by
Boudleaux Bryant and Felice Bryant
Arranged by Melody Bober

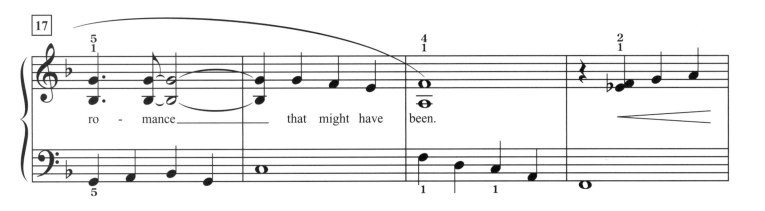

ro - mance_____ that might have been.

Bye   bye   love,   bye   bye   hap - pi - ness,___

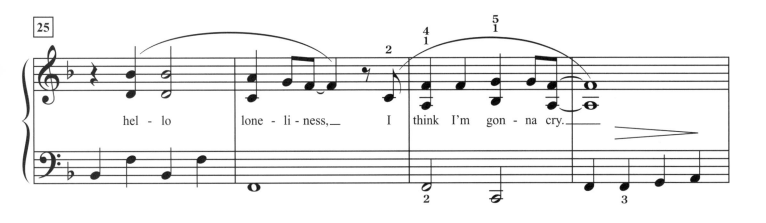

hel - lo   lone - li - ness,___   I   think I'm gon - na cry.___

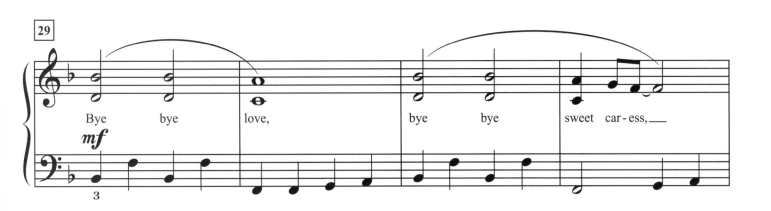

Bye   bye   love,   bye   bye   sweet car - ess,___

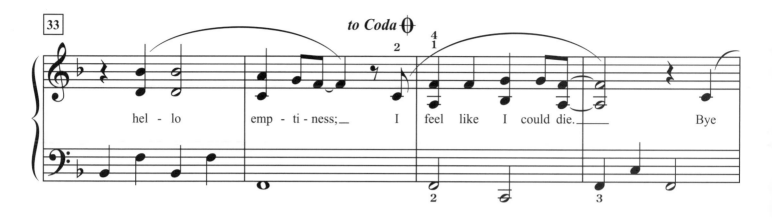

hel - lo emp - ti - ness;__ I feel like I could die.__ Bye

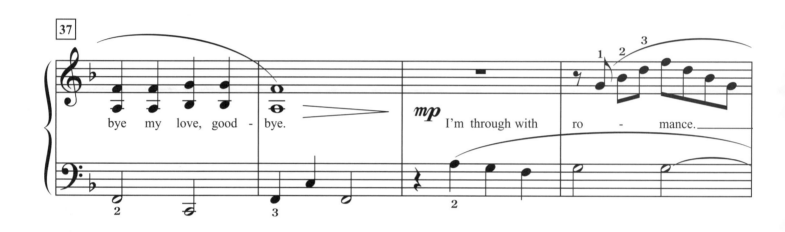

bye my love, good - bye. *mp* I'm through with ro - mance.__

__ I'm through with love.__ I'm through with

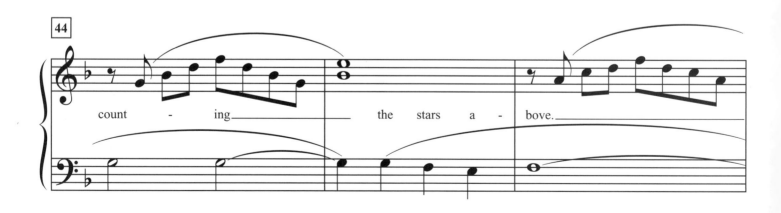

count - ing__ the stars a - bove.__

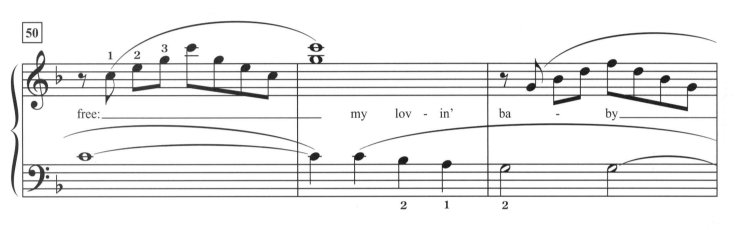

Do You Want to Know a Secret?

Words and Music by
John Lennon and Paul McCartney
Arranged by Melody Bober

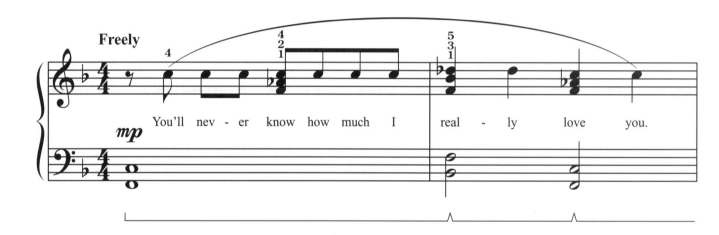

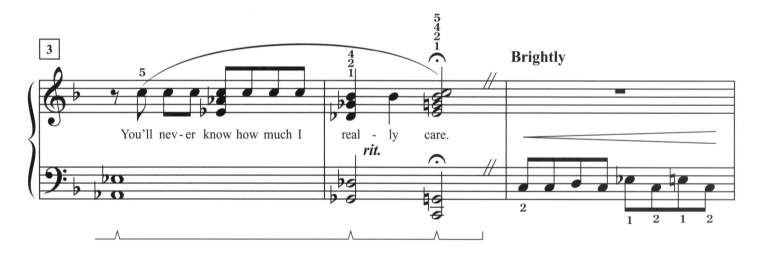

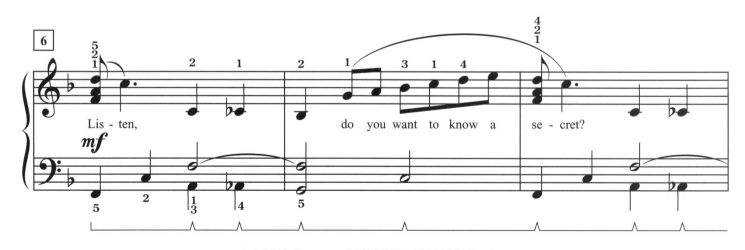

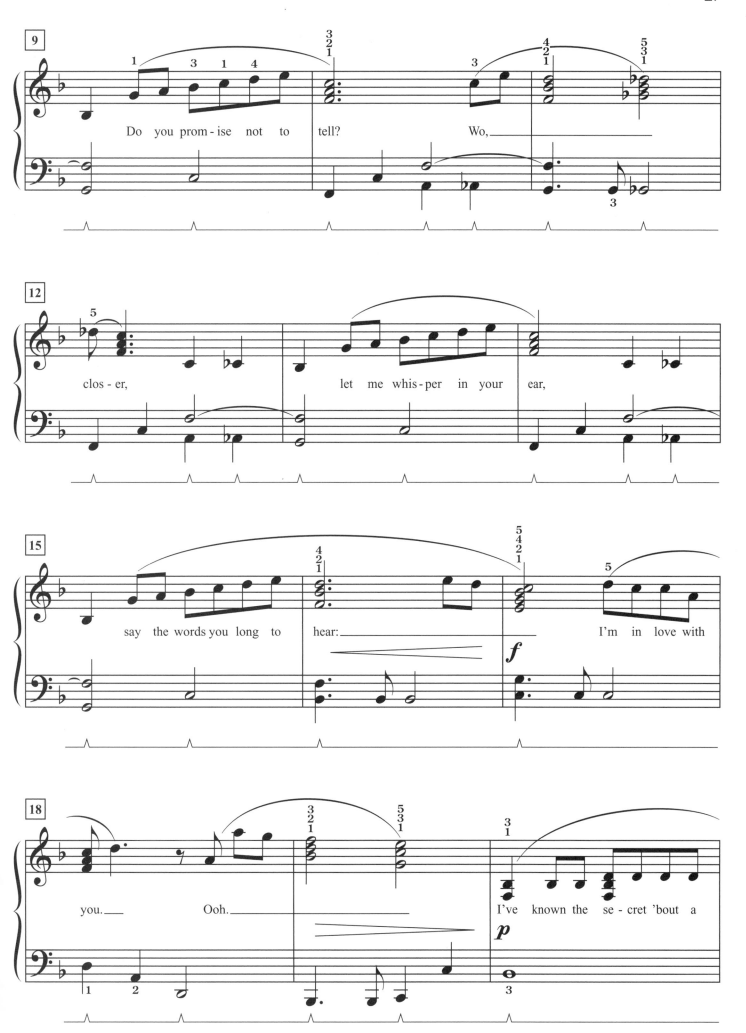

week or two: no - bod - y knows, just we two.

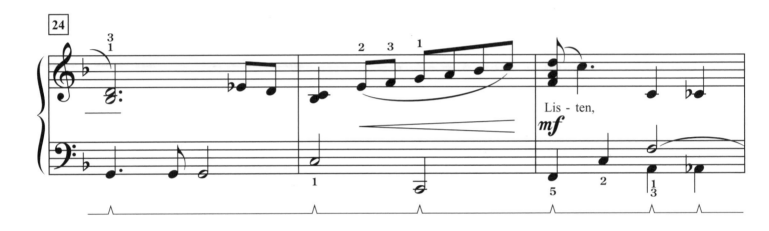

Lis - ten,

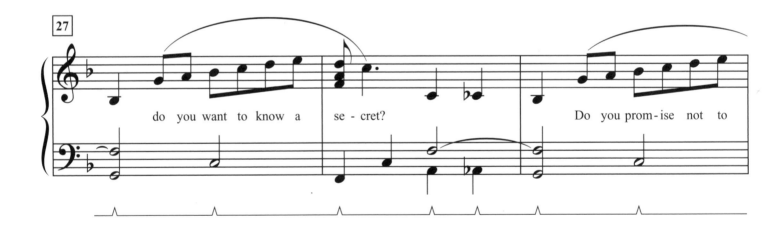

do you want to know a se - cret? Do you prom-ise not to

tell? Wo,_____ clos - er,

Earth Angel

Words and Music by Jesse Belvin
Arranged by Melody Bober

fell_____ for you,_____ and____ I knew_____ the

vi - sion of your love's love - li - ness._____ I

hope_____ and I pray_____ that____ some - day I'll be the

vi - sion of your hap - pi - ness. Earth

I'm Walkin'

Words and Music by
Antoine Domino and Dave Bartholomew
Arranged by Melody Bober

wait - in'___ for your com - pa - ny,___ I'm hop - in'___ that

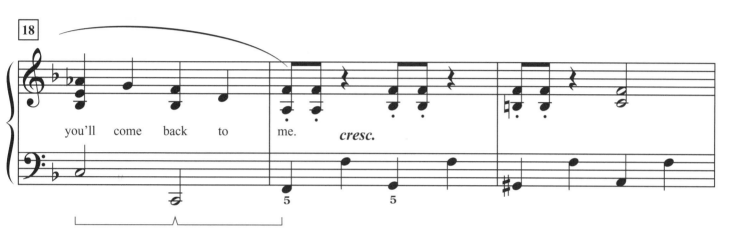

you'll come back to me. *cresc.*

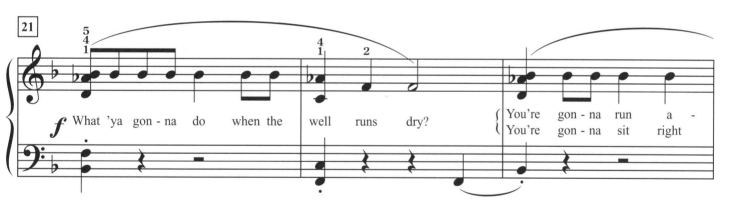

f What 'ya gon - na do when the well runs dry? You're gon - na run a - / You're gon - na sit right

way and hide. I'm gon - na run right by your side, for
down and cry. What 'ya gon - na do when I say "bye bye"?

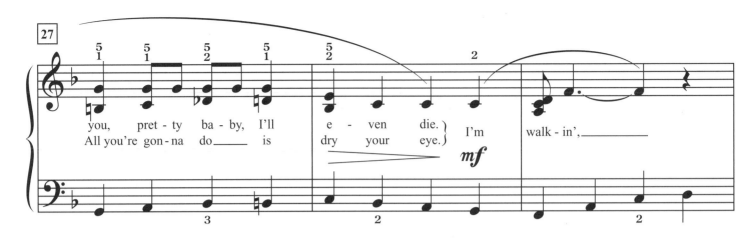

you, pret - ty ba - by, I'll e - ven die.) I'm walk - in', _____
All you're gon - na do ____ is dry your eye.)

mf

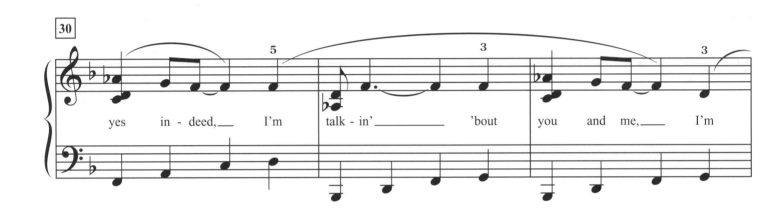

yes in - deed, ____ I'm talk - in' _____ 'bout you and me, ____ I'm

1.

hop - in' _____ that you'll come back to me.

mp

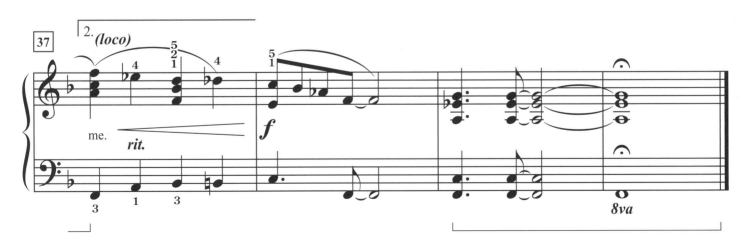

2. *(loco)*

me. *rit.* *f*

8va

It Was a Very Good Year

Words and Music by Ervin Drake
Arranged by Melody Bober

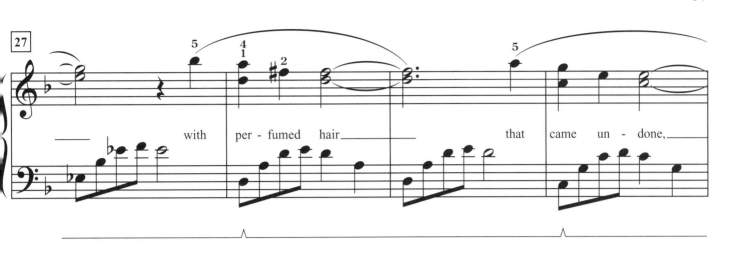

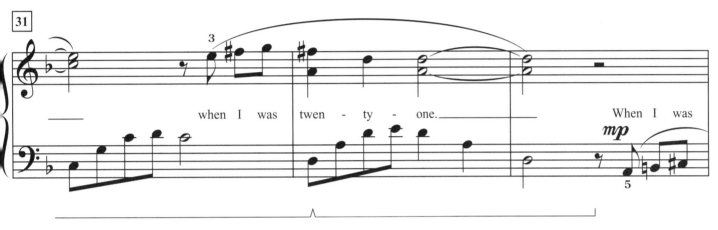

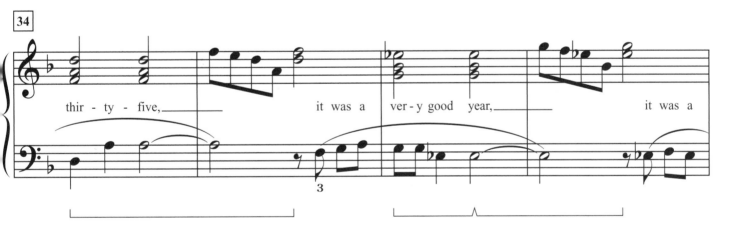

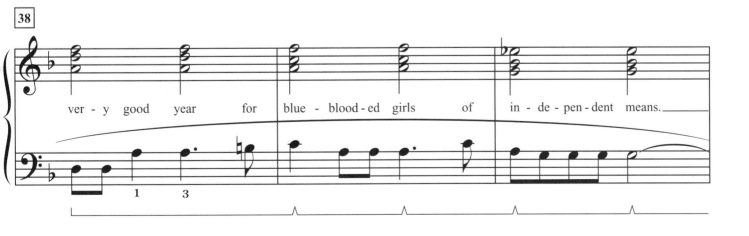

We'd ride in lim-ou-sines. Their

chauf-feurs would drive, when I was thir-ty - five.

But now the days are short.

It's My Party

Words and Music by
Herb Wiener, John Gluck and Wally Gold
Arranged by Melody Bober

It's my par - ty and I'll cry if I want_ to, cry if I want_ to, cry if I want_ to.

You would cry, too, if it hap-pened to you.

Play all my re - cords, keep dan - cing all night,_ but

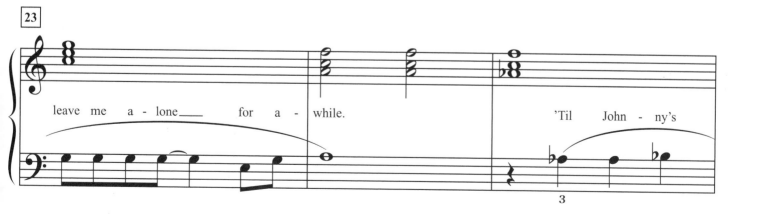

leave me a - lone___ for a - while. 'Til John - ny's

44

walked thru the door,   like a   queen___ with her   king.

D.S. al Coda

Oh,   what   a   birth-day sur-prise,   Ju-dy's wear-ing his   ring.

Coda

sub. p

mf You   would   cry,

too,   if   it   hap-pened   to   you.

f

8va

Itsy Bitsy Teenie Weenie Yellow Polka Dot Bikini

Words and Music by
Paul J. Vance and Lee Pockriss
Arranged by Melody Bober

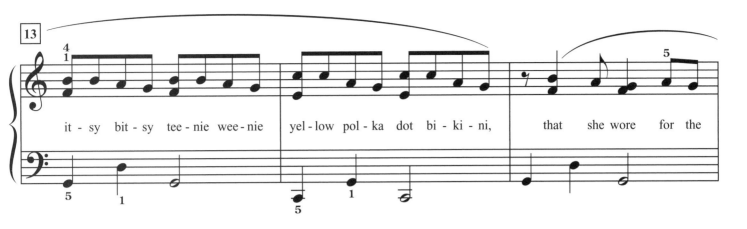

water, and I won - der what she's gon - na do. Now she's a -

fraid to come out of the wa - ter, and the poor lit - tle girl's turn - ing

blue. *Two, three, four,* *tell the peo - ple what she wore.* It was an

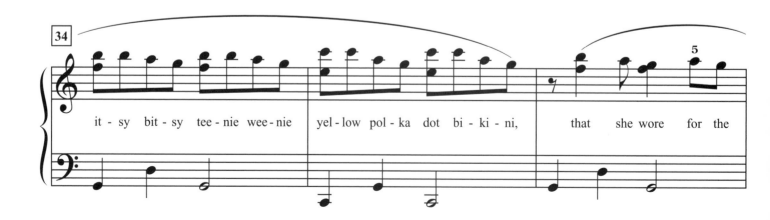

it - sy bit - sy tee - nie wee - nie yel - low pol - ka dot bi - ki - ni, that she wore for the

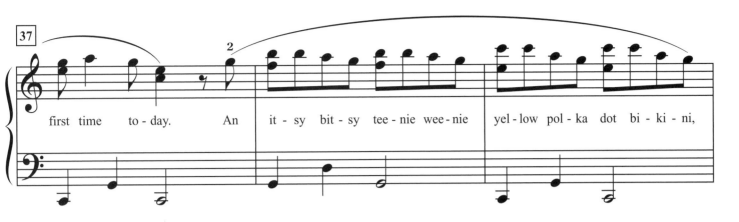

first time to-day. An it-sy bit-sy tee-nie wee-nie yel-low pol-ka dot bi-ki-ni,

so in the lock-er she want-ed to stay. From the lock-er to the

blan-ket, from the blan-ket to the shore. From the shore to the

wa-ter, guess there is-n't an-y more.

The Lion Sleeps Tonight

New Lyric and Revised Music by
George David Weiss, Hugo Peretti and Luigi Creatore
Arranged by Melody Bober

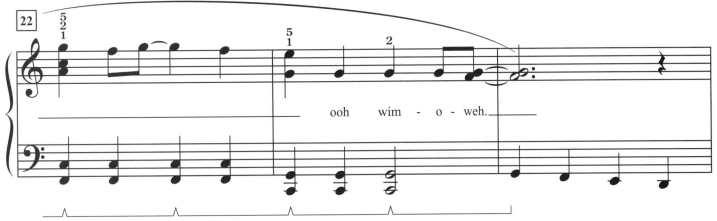

52

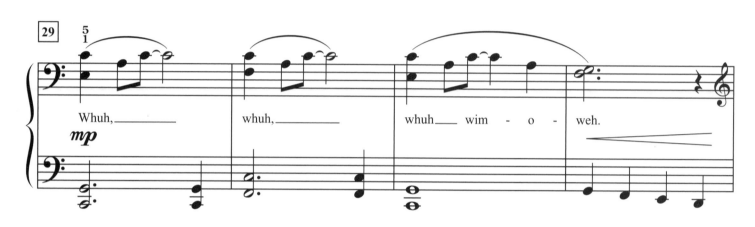

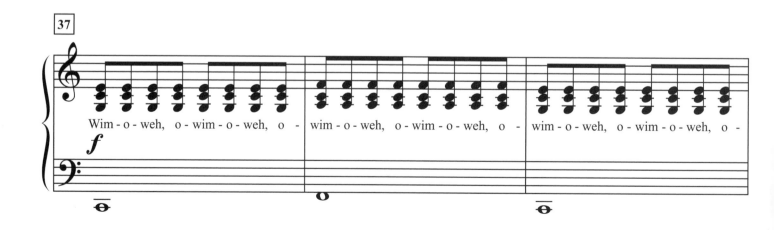

Misty

Words by Johnny Burke
Music by Erroll Garner
Arranged by Melody Bober

56

Mrs. Brown You've Got a Lovely Daughter

Words and Music by Trevor Peacock
Arranged by Melody Bober

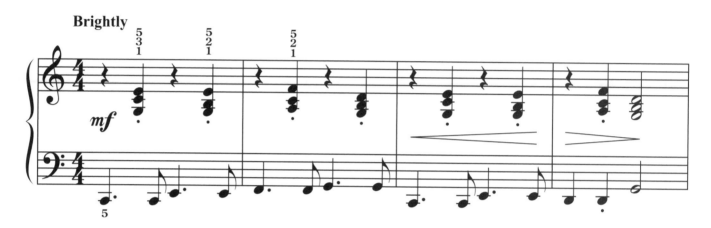

Mis - sis Brown you've got a love - ly daugh - ter.
She wants to re - turn those things I bought her.

Girls as sharp as her are some - thing
Tell her she can keep them just the

60

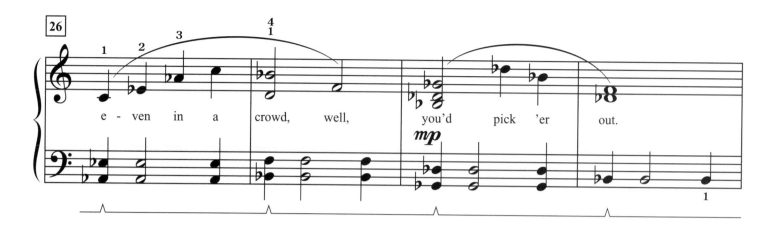

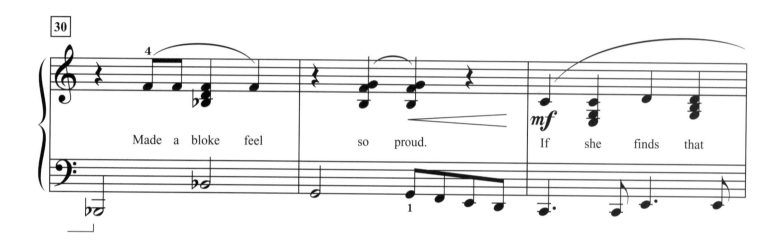

Only You
(And You Alone)

Words and Music by
Buck Ram and Andre Rand
Arranged by Melody Bober

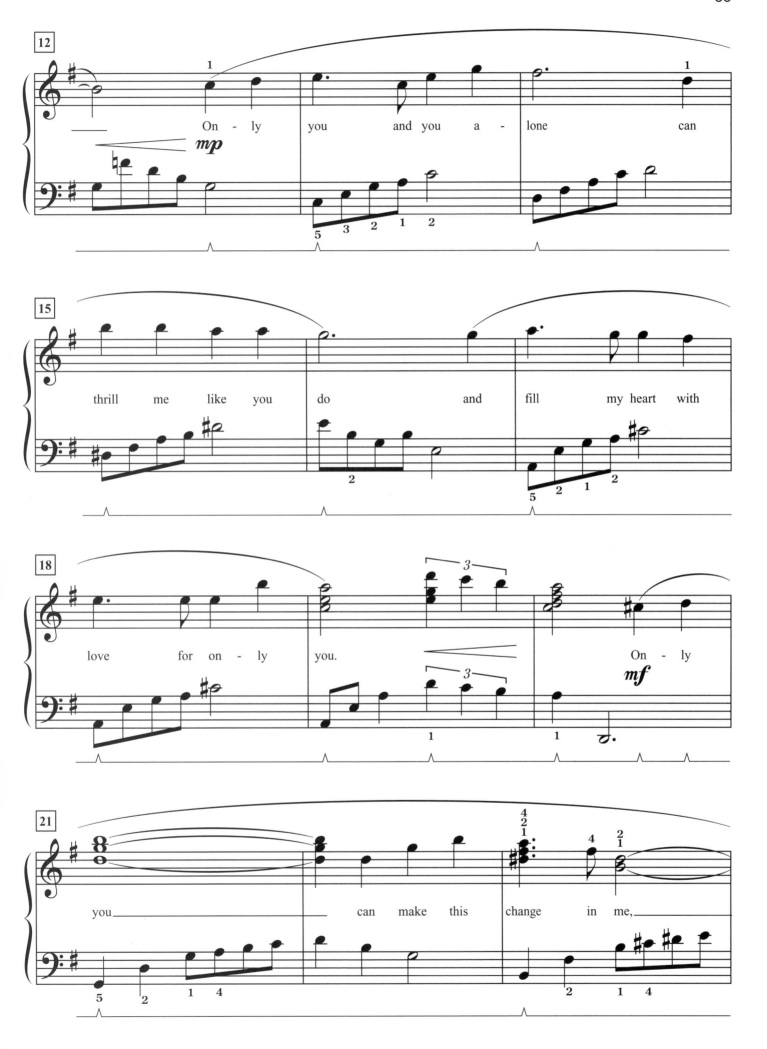

Puff (The Magic Dragon)

Words and Music by
Peter Yarrow and Leonard Lipton
Arranged by Melody Bober

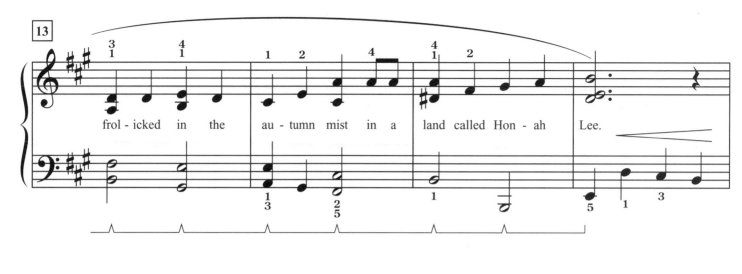

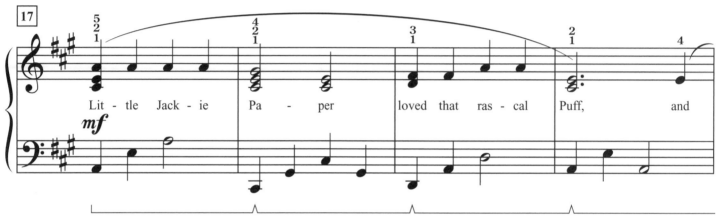

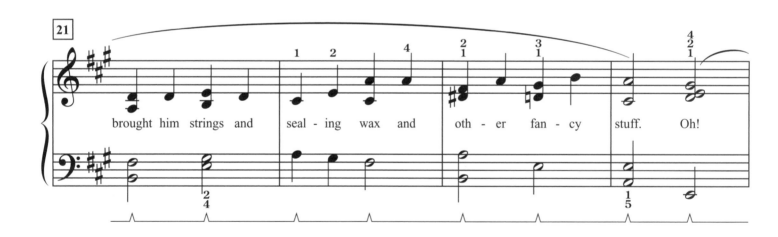

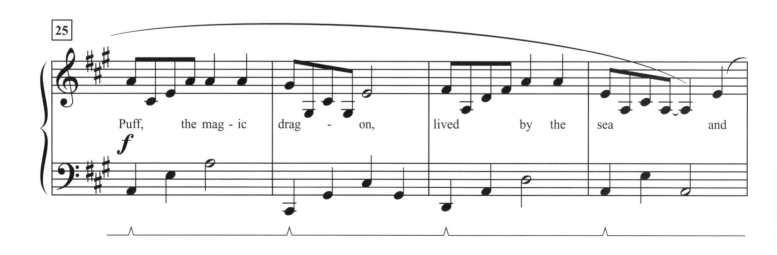

Jack - ie kept a look - out perched on Puff's gi - gan - tic tail.

Nob - le kings and prin - ces would bow when e'er they came.

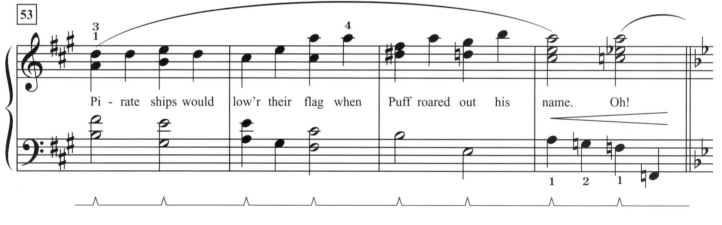

Pi - rate ships would low'r their flag when Puff roared out his name. Oh!

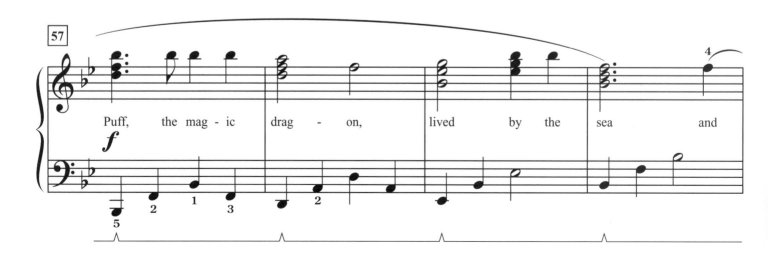

Puff, the mag - ic drag - on, lived by the sea and

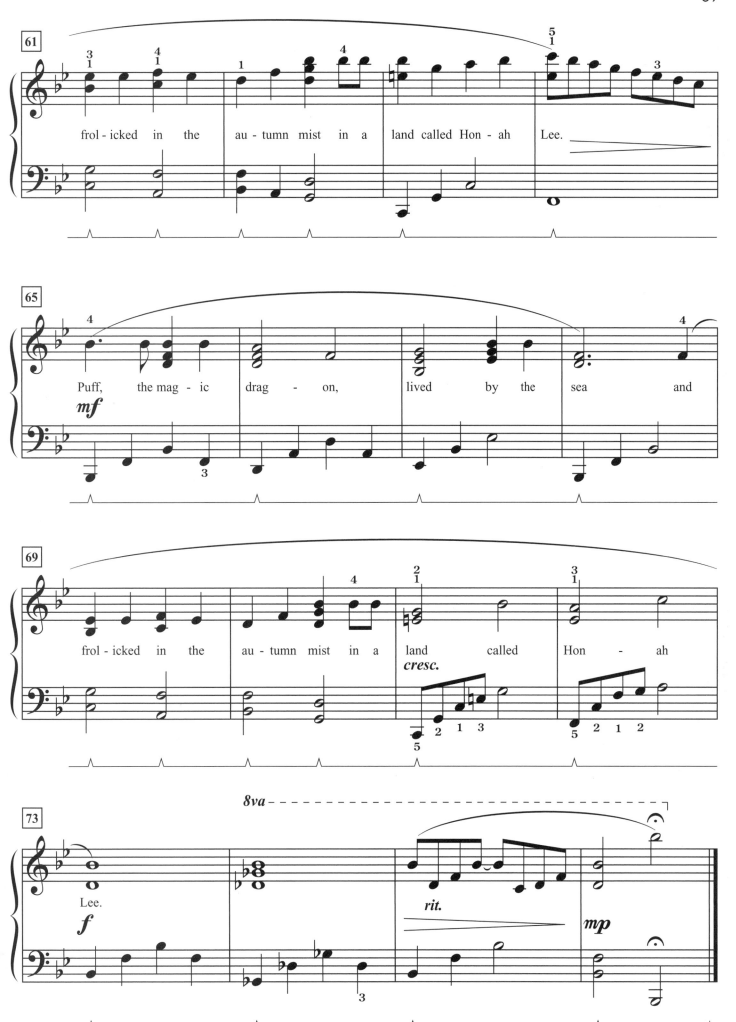

(We're Gonna) Rock Around the Clock

Words and Music by
Max C. Freedman and Jimmy DeKnight
Arranged by Melody Bober

clock strikes two and three and four,__ if the band slows down, we'll
chimes ring five and six and sev'n,__ we'll be rock-in' up in

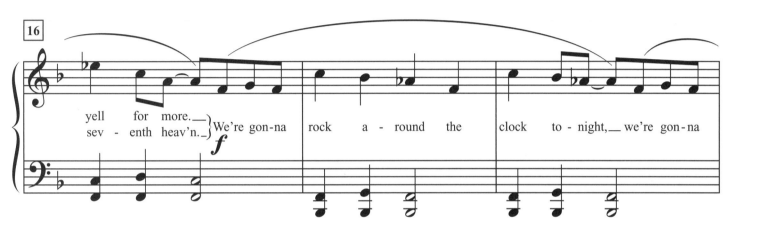

yell for more.__ } We're gon-na rock a-round the clock to-night,__ we're gon-na
sev-enth heav'n.__ } *f*

rock, rock, rock 'til broad day-light.__ We're gon-na rock, gon-na rock a-

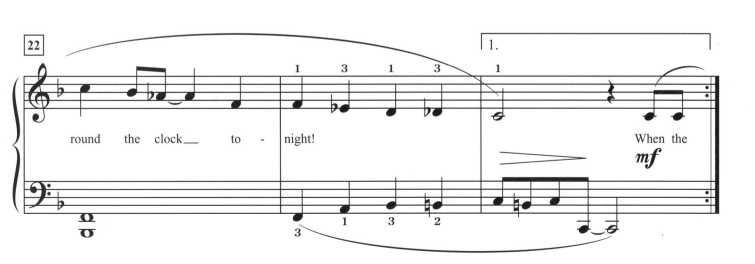

round the clock__ to - night!

When the
mf

Runaround Sue

Words and Music by
Dion DiMucci and Ernest Maresca
Arranged by Melody Bober

76

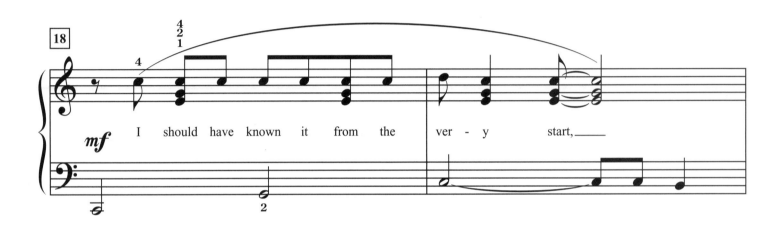

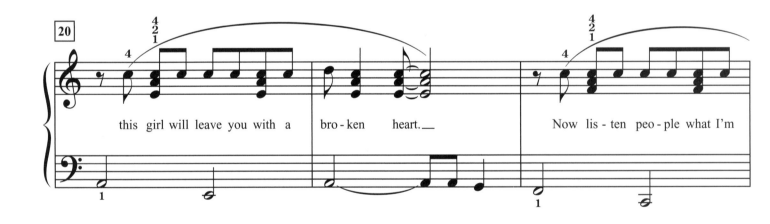

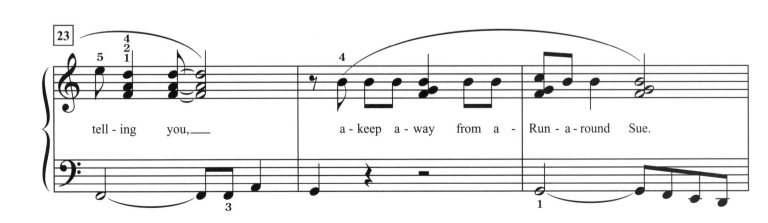

I miss her lips and the smile on her face,___ the touch of her hair and this

girl's warm em - brace.___ So if you don't wan-na cry___ like I do,___

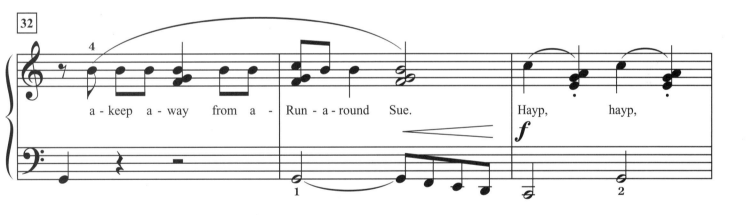

a - keep a - way from a - Run - a - round Sue. Hayp, hayp,

bum-da ha-dy, ha-dy, hayp, hayp, bum-da ha-dy, ha-dy, hayp, hayp,

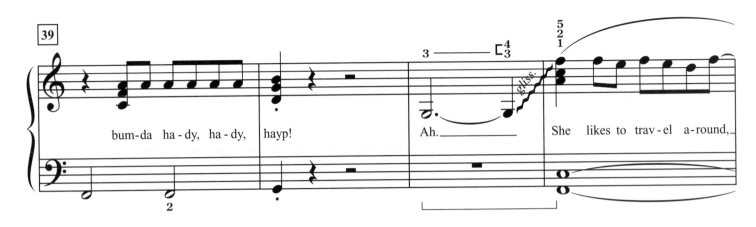

bum-da ha-dy, ha-dy, hayp! Ah._____ She likes to trav-el a-round,

she'll love you but she'll put___ you down.___ Now

peo-ple let me put you wise,_____ Sue goes

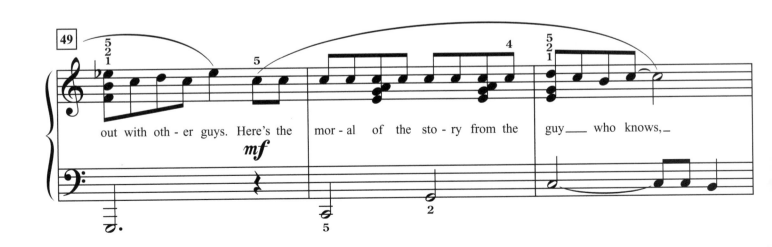

out with oth-er guys. Here's the mor-al of the sto-ry from the guy___ who knows,___

I fell in love and my love still grows.__ Ask an-y fool that

she ev-er knew,__ they'll say keep a-way from a - Run - a -round Sue.

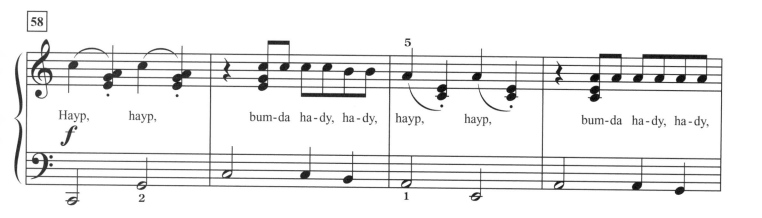

Hayp, hayp, bum-da ha-dy, ha-dy, hayp, hayp, bum-da ha-dy, ha-dy,

hayp, hayp, bum-da ha-dy, ha-dy, hayp!

Runaway

Words and Music by
Del Shannon and Max Crook
Arranged by Melody Bober

why, why, why, why, why she ran a - way. ___ And __ I won - der

where she will stay, ___ my lit - tle run - a - way,

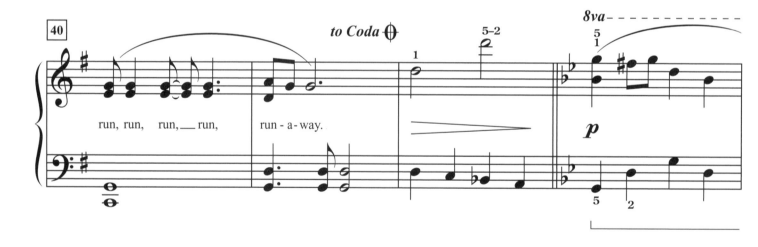

run, run, run, ___ run, run - a - way.

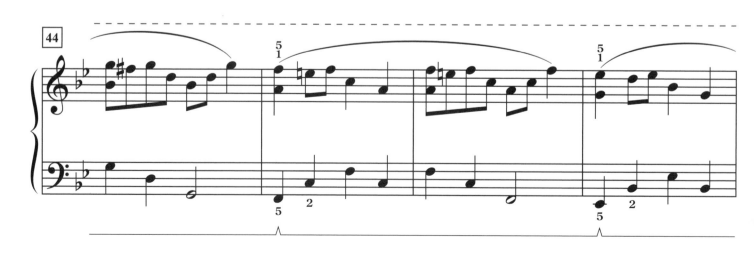

Save the Last Dance for Me

Words by Doc Pomus
Music by Mort Shuman
Arranged by Melody Bober

Shake, Rattle and Roll

Words and Music by Charles E. Calhoun
Arranged by Melody Bober

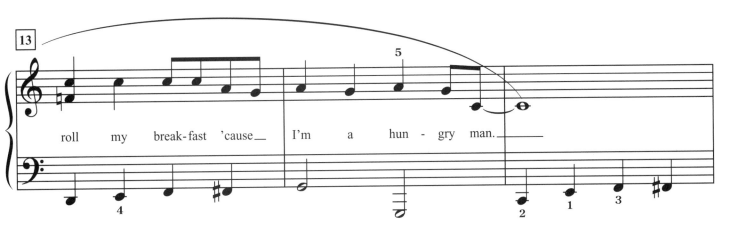

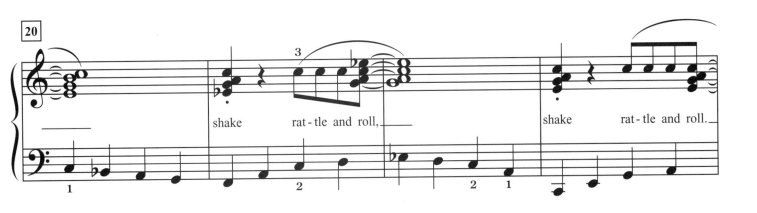

28

Wear-in' those dress-es, your hair done up so right,

mp

32

wear-in' those dress-es, your hair done up so right.

36

You look so warm,___ but your heart is cold___ as ice.

mf

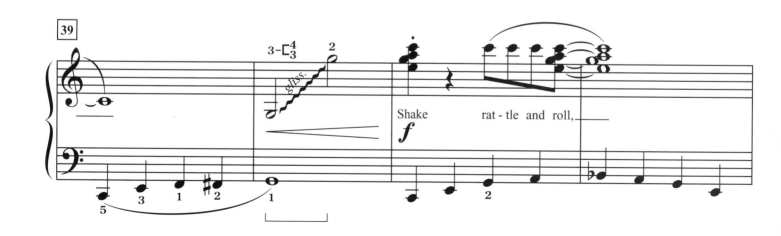

39

Shake rat - tle and roll,___

f

shake rat - tle and roll,_____ shake rat - tle and roll,_

_____ shake rat - tle and roll._____ You

nev - er do noth - in' to save your dog - gone soul.

Sixteen Candles

Words and Music by
Luther Dixon and Allyson Khent
Arranged by Melody Bober

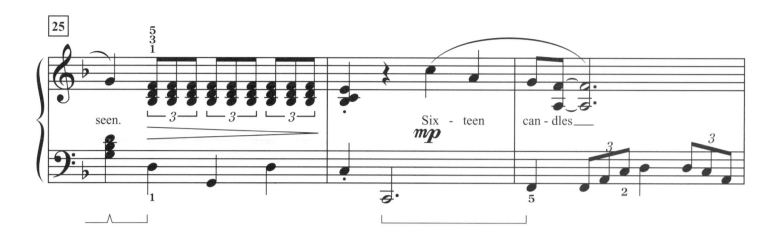

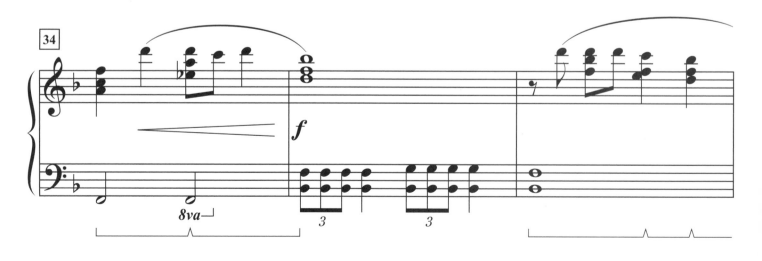

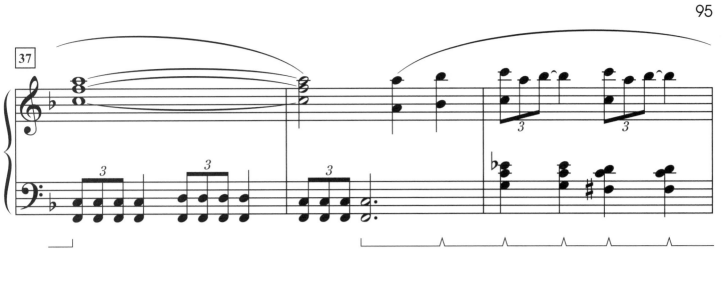

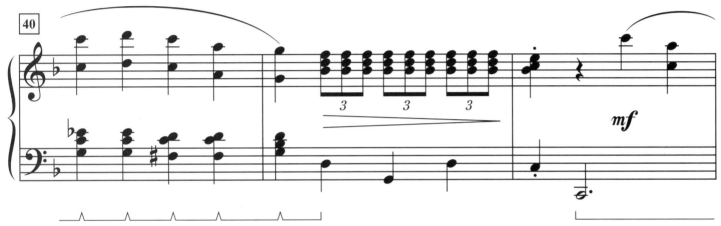

Splish Splash

Words and Music by
Bobby Darin and Jean Murray
Arranged by Melody Bober

stepped out the tub, put my feet on the floor, I wrapped the towel a-round me and I

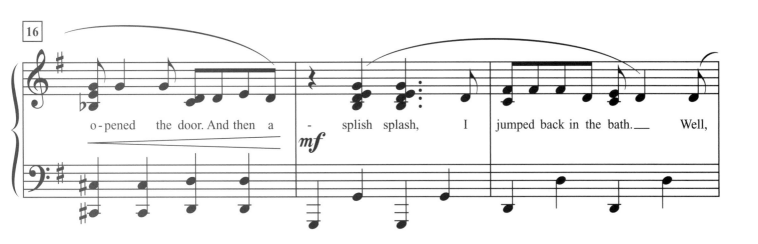

o-pened the door. And then a - splish splash, I jumped back in the bath.___ Well,

mf

how was I to know there was a par-ty go-ing on? Bing bang, I

saw the whole gang___ danc-in' on my liv-in' room rug.

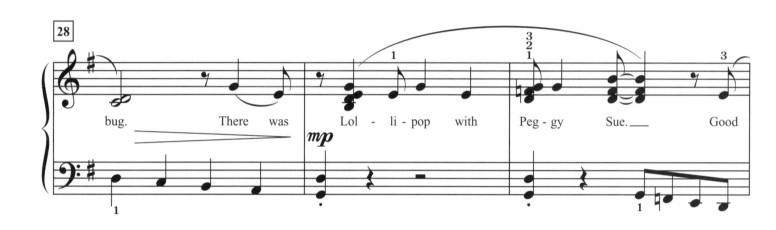

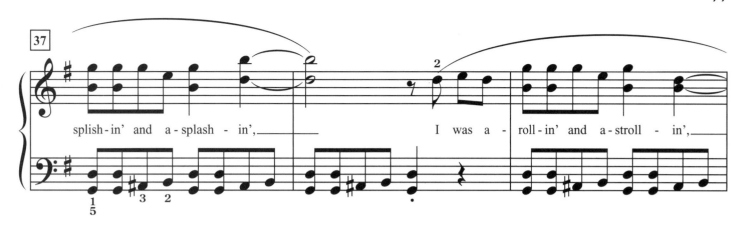

splish-in' and a-splash-in', I was a-roll-in' and a-stroll-in',

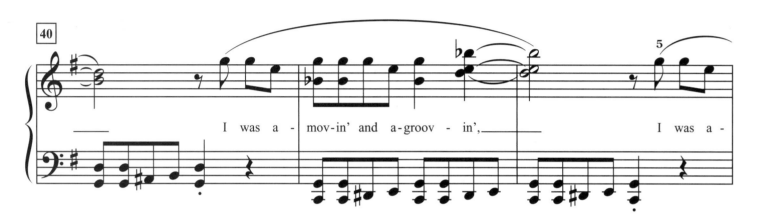

I was a-mov-in' and a-groov-in', I was a-

reel-in' with the feel-in'.

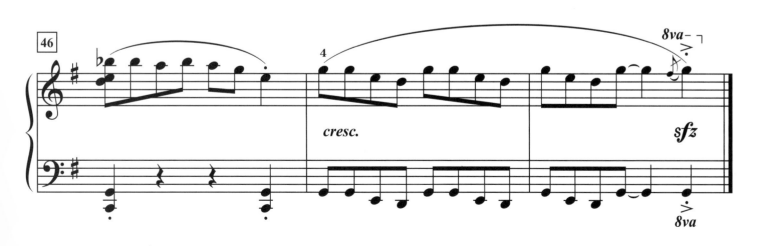

cresc. sfz

A Teenager In Love

Words by Doc Pomus
Music by Mort Shuman
Arranged by Melody Bober

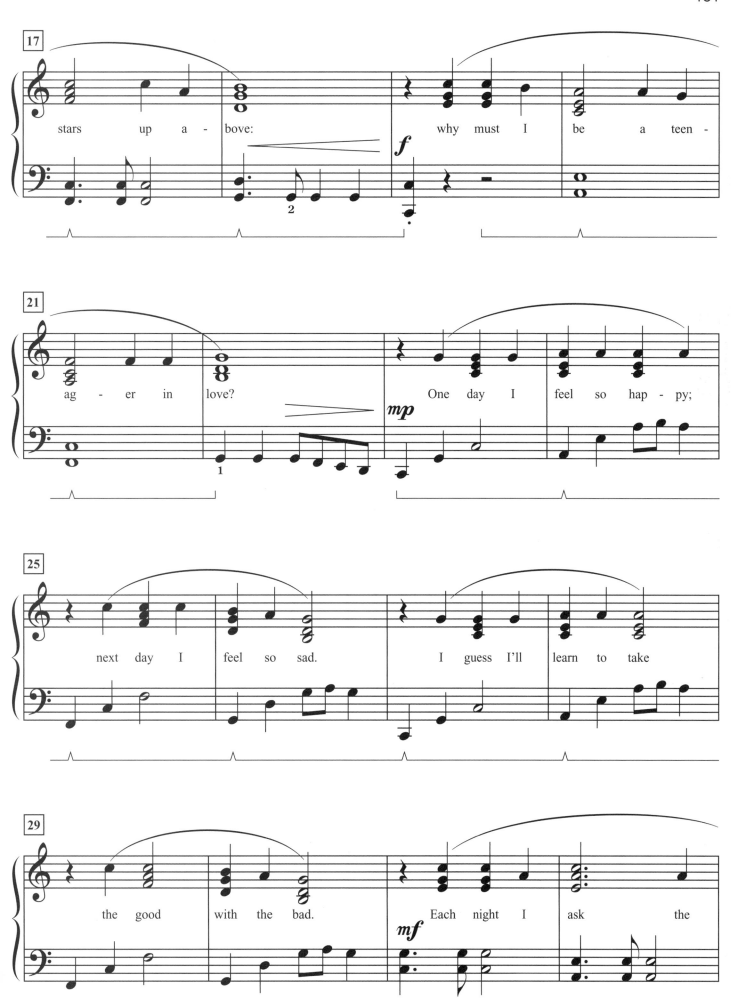

stars up a - bove: why must I be a teen -

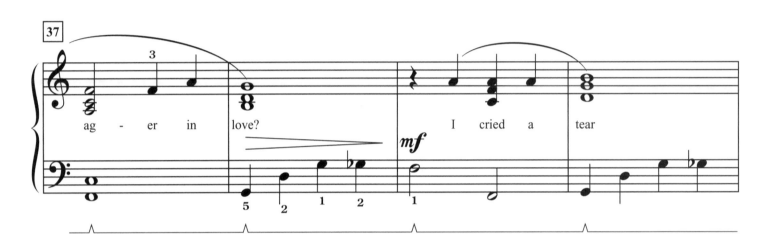

ag - er in love? I cried a tear

for no - bod - y but you. I'll be a lone - ly one if

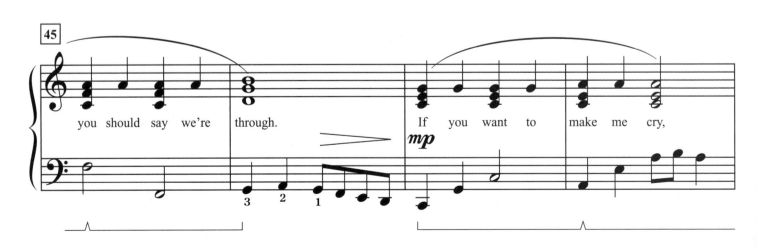

you should say we're through. If you want to make me cry,

Wipe Out

By The Surfaris
Arranged by Melody Bober

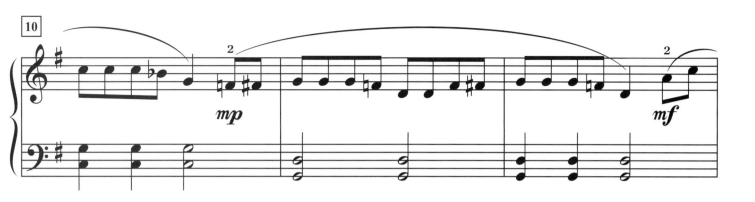

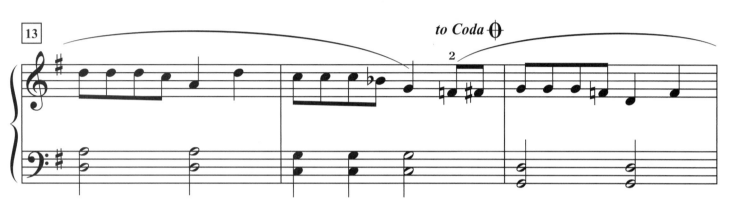

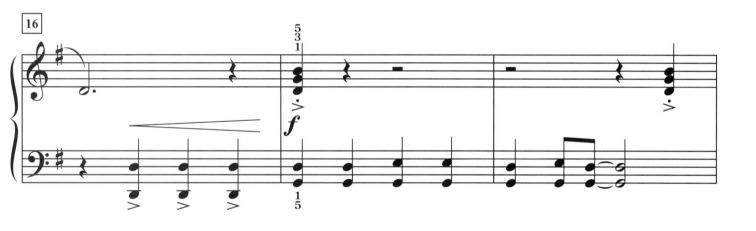

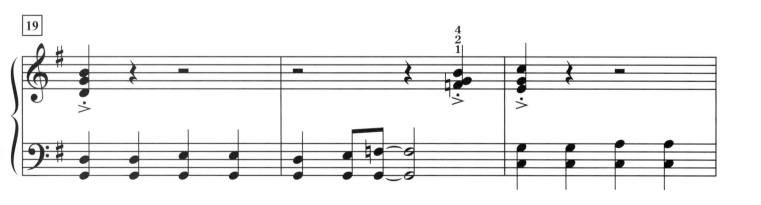

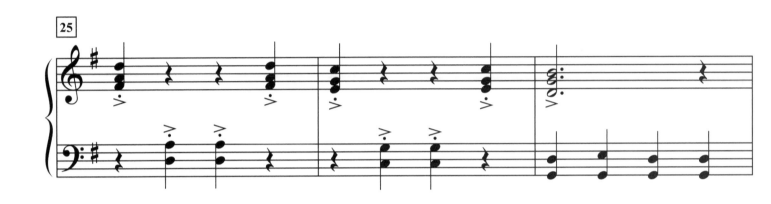

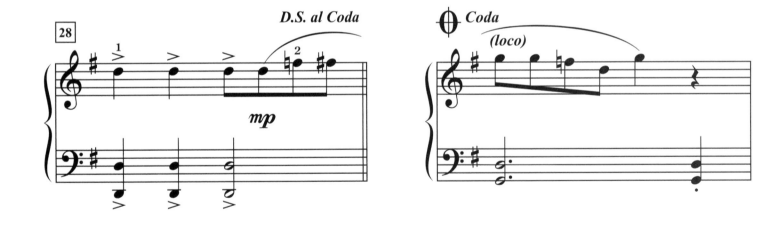